NICARAGUA

NICARAGUA

JUNE 1978 – JULY 1979

SUSAN MEISELAS

EDITED WITH CLAIRE ROSENBERG

PANTHEON BOOKS, NEW YORK

Grateful acknowledgment is made to the following for permission to
reprint previously published material:

Editorial Laia for permission to translate into English an excerpt from
Antologia by Ernesto Cardenal, Editorial Laia, Barcelona, 3d. ed.,
February 1980.

Library of Congress Cataloging in Publication Data
Meiselas, Susan.
Nicaragua.
1. Nicaragua — History — Revolution, 1979 — Pictorial works.
F1528.M44   972.85′052   80-7700
ISBN 0-394-51265-0
ISBN 0-394-73931-0 (pbk.)

A C K N O W L E D G M E N T S

Thanks to Gilles, who introduced me to Peter, with whom I
met Miguel, and thereby came to know Nicaragua and to know
Carlos, Justo, Lea, Sylvia, Julio, Margarita, Dionisio, Damian,
René, Fabian, Ocho, Omar, Joaquín, Alvaro, Sergio. . . . The
making of this book owes special thanks to Kay and Robert
for continuing support; to Julia and Fae for reading again and
again; to Danny, Nancy, Sally believing it would come; to
Pierre, Alan, Francis, Andy rendering it better. To Claire who
persisted; to Alma for perspective; to Carol and Edmundo who
always stood by. Finally to André who waited.

And to the Nicaraguan people for whom waiting meant fifty
years. . . .

Typographic design by Susan Mitchell

Manufactured in the United States of America
First Edition

Ni me voy ni me van. . . .

I'll neither go nor be driven out. . .

> –*Anastasio Somoza Debayle,*
> *president of Nicaragua*
> *November 1978*

An unarmed people's war is nothing like a military coup. It is a war of attrition, long and silent. Many have fallen. Thousands of its actions remain unknown. The news tells only of those that are most important.

This is not something that started with these last offensives. We who live this struggle know that day by day there are confrontations, something happens. It is a long history, like building a house, stone by stone. . . .

> –*German Pomares,*
> *FSLN commander,*
> *died in combat May 28, 1979, in Jinotega*

It was like putting on the final reel of a war movie. A violent and bloody end seemed inevitable to everyone. And we all accepted it as our immediate fate. No one was prepared to say "no" to violence if the alternative was the perpetuation of Somoza.

> –*Managua lawyer*

This government has no moral authority to govern.

The cause of the problem is the rule of the Somoza family. They have turned the National Guard into a private army.

The strike was a desperate attempt to overthrow Somoza. After the strike there was a sense of frustration in the private sector. They suddenly felt weaker than they thought they were. The government has lost all control, so much so that even primary school students are on strike.

We don't know where we are going. We don't know what is next. What we are living now is a form of civil war.

> –*Jaime Montealegre Lacayo, economist,*
> *heir of the second wealthiest family in Nicaragua*

JUNE 1978

THE SOMOZA REGIME

SEPTEMBER 1978

INSURRECTION

JUNE 1979 – JULY 1979

THE FINAL OFFENSIVE

NICARAGUA.
A year of news,
as if nothing had happened before,
as if the roots were not there,
and the victory not earned.

This book was made
so that we remember.

– S.C.M. July 1980

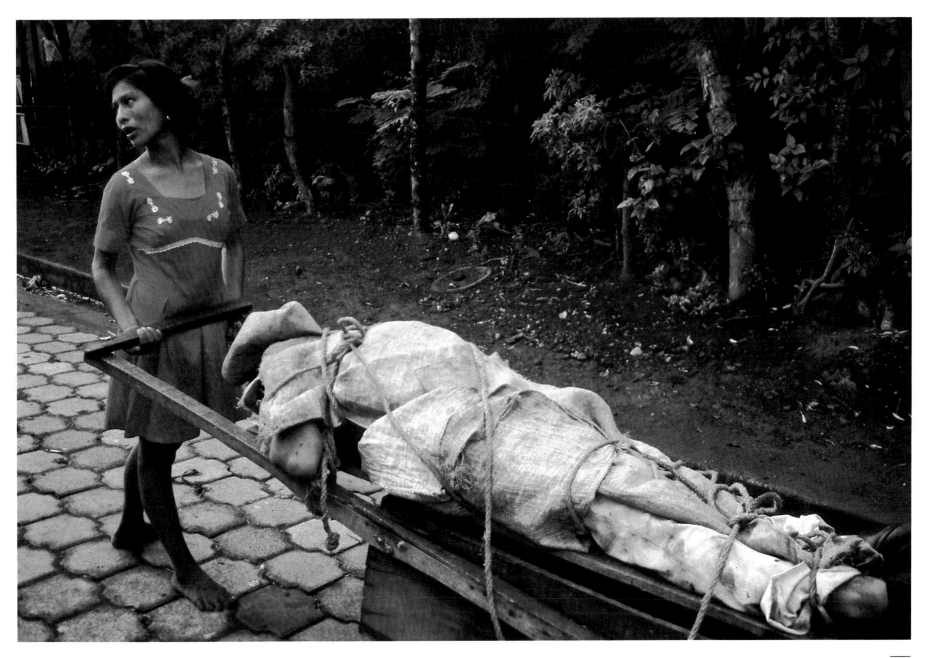

CAPTIONS

TEXTS

CHRONOLOGY

With lies they tried to make us lie.
As if they did not know
that the mouth was made to say
the eyes see . . .

*–Peasants speaking at a
meeting, Matagalpa, August 1975*

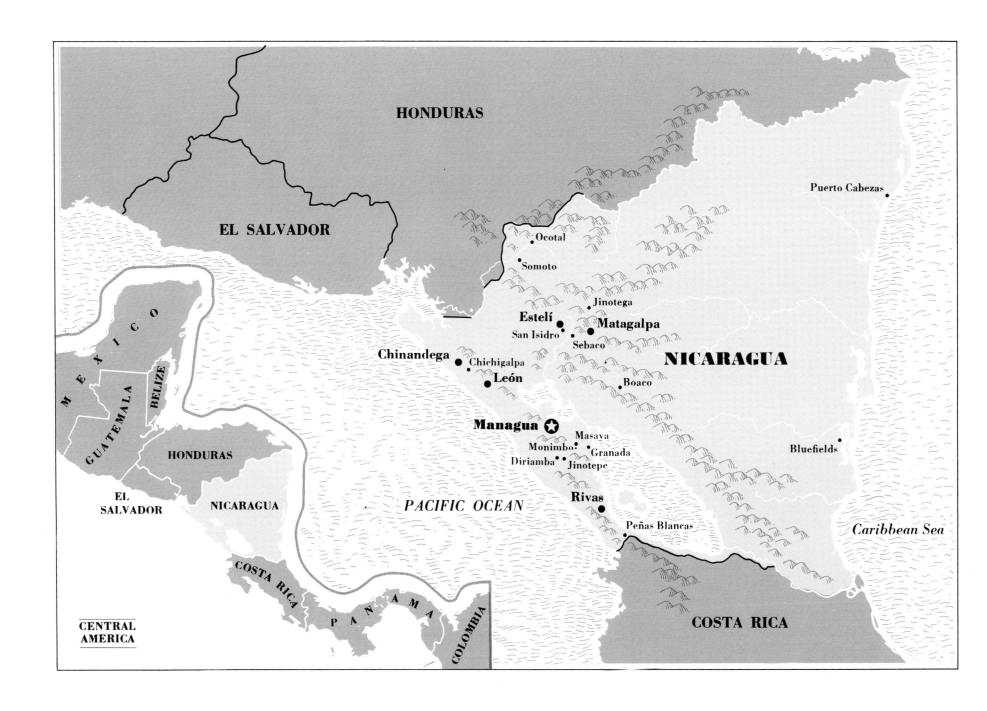

HONDURAS

EL SALVADOR

Puerto Cabezas

Ocotal

Somoto

Jinotega

Estelí **Matagalpa**

San Isidro
Sebaco

NICARAGUA

Chinandega Chichigalpa

León Boaco

Managua ⭐

Masaya
Monimbo Granada
Diriamba Jinotepe

Bluefields

Rivas

Peñas Blancas

PACIFIC OCEAN

Caribbean Sea

COSTA RICA

MEXICO

GUATEMALA

BELIZE

HONDURAS

EL
SALVADOR

NICARAGUA

COSTA RICA

PANAMA

COLOMBIA

**CENTRAL
AMERICA**

1 8 9 0

The construction of the Nicaraguan canal will secure the domination of the United States over the American Continent, politically as well as commercially. . . . The nation that, with the Nicaraguan Government on a joint agreement, controls Lake Nicaragua, will then control the destiny of the Western Hemisphere. . . .

– *William L. Merry,*
American minister to Nicaragua

C H A M O R R O - B R Y A N   T R E A T Y

Signed: June 22, 1916

The government of Nicaragua grants in perpetuity to the government of the United States, forever free from all taxation or other public charge, the exclusive proprietary rights necessary and convenient for the construction, operation, and maintenance of an interoceanic canal by way of the San Juan River and great Lake of Nicaragua or by way of any route over Nicaraguan territory . . . [for] the sum of $3 million U.S. gold coin, of the present weight and fineness. . . .

– *U.S. Department of State,*
Publication No. 8642

1 9 2 6

I said to my friends that if there were a hundred men in Nicaragua who loved their country as much as I, we would redeem its sovereignty, now endangered by the Yankee empire. My friends replied that there might be that many men, or even more, but the problem would lie in our finding each other. . . .

1 9 2 7

I am not prepared to surrender my weapons even if everybody else does. I would rather be killed along with the few who accompany me, because it is better to die as rebels under fire than to live as slaves. . . .

– *Augusto César Sandino,*
leader of the peasant army

1

Traditional Indian dance mask from the town of Monimbo, adopted by the rebels during the fight against Somoza to conceal identity.

2

Main street of rural town, Santo Domingo

3

Woman washing laundry in sewer of downtown Managua.

Harvesting sugar cane near León

*Loading one hundred pound
sacks of grain, Granada*

Country club, Managua

N I C A R A G U A *

POPULATION:	2.2 million
GOVERNMENT:	Ruled by the Somoza family since 1936
RELIGION:	90% Roman Catholic
LAND:	5% of population owned 58% of arable land; Somoza family owned 23%.
WEALTH:	50% of population had an average annual income of $90.
UNEMPLOYMENT:	Officially 22%, but unemployment affected 60% of the population
ILLITERACY:	57% nationwide, but 80% average in rural areas
HOUSING:	80% had no running water, 59% no electricity, 47% no sanitary facilities, 69% dirt floors.
HEALTH:	Endemic malaria, tuberculosis, typhoid, and gastroenteritis. Of every 1000 children born, 102 died. Of every 10 deaths, 6 were of infectious diseases, which are curable.

*These statistics were compiled from the U.S. Agency for
International Development, 1971 Nicaraguan census, U.N.
Economic Commission for Latin America, and Central
American Permanent Secretariat for Economic Integration,
among other sources. However, it should be noted that reliable
up-to-date statistics were impossible to obtain under the
Somoza regime.

(. . .)

*The great-grandparents of the people of
Acahualinca were less hungry than their
grandparents.*

The great-grandparents died of hunger.

*The grandparents of the people of Acahualinca
were less hungry than their parents.*

The grandparents died of hunger.

*The parents of the people of Acahualinca
were less hungry than the children of the
people of that place.*

The parents died of hunger.

*The people of Acahualinca are less hungry
than the children of the people of that place.*

*The children of the people of Acahualinca
are not born because of hunger,*

and hunger to be born, to die of hunger.

*– Excerpt from poem by Leonel Rugama,
"The Earth is a Satellite of the Moon."
Seminary student and member of the Sandinista
National Liberation Front (FSLN), who died
fighting in Managua, January 15, 1970*

TELEGRAM

SENOR GENERAL ANASTASIO SOMOZA DEBAYLE
HEAD OF THE NATIONAL GUARD
SUPREME COMMANDER OF THE ARMED FORCES
PRESIDENT OF THE NATIONAL EMERGENCY COMMITTEE
PRESIDENT OF THE AGRICULTURAL COMMITTEE
DELEGATE TO THE CENTRAL AMERICAN COMMON MARKET
LEADER OF THE NATIONAL LIBERAL PARTY
HEAD OF THE FOREIGN FINANCE COMMITTEE
CANDIDATE FOR THE PRESIDENCY OF THE REPUBLIC
EX-PRESIDENT OFTHE REPUBLIC
GRAND MASTER OF THE ORDER "RUBEN DARIO"
SENATOR FOR LIFE
PROMOTER OF RURAL ELECTRIFICATION
PROMOTER OF AGRO-INDUSTRY
PRESIDENT OF LANICA AIRLINES
PRESIDENT OF MAMENIC SHIPPING LINE
CHAIRMAN OF THE NATIONAL CEMENT COMPANY
CHIEF EXECUTIVE OF "EL PORVENIR" PLANTATION
CHIEF EXECUTIVE OF "CENTRAL DE INGENIOS" REFINERIES

LEADER, FLAGBEARER, PROMINENT ONE, GUIDE, INSPIRED
AND ILLUSTRIOUS ONE, SAVIOR, SUPREME RULER,
BENEFACTOR, UNIQUE LEADER, GLORIOUS ONE, TALENTED
ONE, MAN OF DESTINY, COUNSELLOR, ILLUMINATOR, WISE,
VIRTUOUS, UPSTANDING, INSPIRING, INTELLIGENT, REGAL,
SERENE, PRUDENT, BUILDER, CREATOR, HURRICANE OF
PEACE, NEGOTIATOR, FUTURE PRESIDENT, REFEREE,
ARBITER OF JUSTICE, SUPREME COMMANDER, GENERAL IN
CHIEF, FAMOUS ONE, MAGNANIMOUS AND GENEROUS ONE,
HIS EXCELLENCY, MOST EXCELLENT ONE, JUDGE,
PREDESTINED, DISTINGUISHED, RENOWNED, CHOSEN,
VICTORIOUS, BRILLIANT, STRONG PERSONALITY, CLEVER,
FABULOUS, MAGNETIC, WEST POINTER, STRATEGIST,
ORGANIZER, PROTECTOR, STATESMAN, COMFORTER OF
THE AFFLICTED, STATISTICIAN, WINNER, SWORD, PACIFIER,
POLAR STAR, MORNING STAR, GENIUS, RESTORER,

EMANCIPATOR, LIBERATOR, IDEALIST, LIBERAL, PLANNER,
SOLID ACADEMIC BACKGROUND, MAN OF SCIENCE,
ENGINEER, HELMSMAN, PILOT, CAPTAIN, DIRECTOR OF
INDUSTRY, BASTION, BULWARK, FORTRESS, BEACON, THE
MAN, PALADIN, PATRIOT, DEMOCRAT, SAVIOR OF THE
REPUBLIC, GIANT, FIRST TAXI DRIVER (AND ALL "FIRSTS"
EVER KNOWN OR IMAGINABLE), SACRIFICED TO HIS
PEOPLE, ALTRUISTIC, DOCTOR HONORIS CAUSA, BACHELOR
AD HONOREM, CHIEF OF CHIEFS, INDISPUTABLE CHIEF,
SUSTENANCE OF DEMOCRACY, SUPPORTER OF LATIN
AMERICA AND GREAT FRIEND OF NIXON

Señor General:

We read all these descriptions of you in your own newspaper, *Novedades*, and have been underlining them every day up until Monday last, August 12.

In the name of any of these offices or qualities, we would like to ask you to do something to stop the price of consumer goods from increasing, and to make the rain fall.

Your humble servants, workers of the city of Managua,

Antonio García, F. Cruz, H. Martinez

—Telegram published August 1973 in La Prensa, *a Managua daily newspaper run by leaders of the moderate opposition and owned by Pedro Joaquín Chamorro.*

President Anastasio Somoza Debayle opening new session of the National Congress, June 1978

Anastasio Somoza Portocarrero, twenty-seven-year-old son of the president, head of the elite infantry training school (EEBI). Following a tradition of the United States Army, the recruits celebrate graduation with Schlitz beer.

New recruits to National Guard practice blindfolded dismantling of a U.S.-made M-16 rifle

10

Children harassing Guards around bonfire in Matagalpa, June 1978

11

Recruits pass by official state portrait of Anastasio Somoza Debayle as President and Commander-in-Chief of the Armed Forces.

12

National Guard on duty in Matagalpa

Our fathers, they have been humiliated. They have suffered this dictatorship all their lives. They drink to forget. . . . They did what they could, but nothing changed.

–Julio,
fourteen-year-old boy of Matagalpa

Perhaps you enlisted in the National Guard because you were unemployed. You were probably without land, with no place to work. Or a farm laborer tired of working for almost nothing. So you decided to try the National Guard. Or perhaps you were simply so hungry, they talked you into it.

Now Somoza and the rich of this country are using you as cannon fodder, turning you against your own people. You, the enlisted men, are the guard dogs who watch over the riches of Somoza and the wealthy. That is why they praise you. We appeal to your conscience: think about this, and compare the lives of your superiors to those of the peasants and workers they send you to kill.

– Letter signed by the FSLN
and sent to the National Guard
September 1975

We are anguished by the suffering of our people, urban and peasant, rich and poor, civilian and military, beg God to protect their lives and their right to enjoy the fruits of their labor. Unfortunately, much of the suffering is provoked by our own Nicaraguan brothers. We report the situation without political objectives in the hope of converting all those committed to seeking peace:

—the state of terror obliges many of our peasants to flee desperately from their homes and land, many villages have been practically abandoned;
—accusations and subsequent arbitrary arrests continue provoking intranquility;
—investigations of suspects involve humiliation and inhumane methods, from torture and rape to summary execution, without civil and military trial;
—in some areas, army patrols have used Catholic chapels as barracks and some lay preachers have been captured by the army and tortured, others have disappeared. . . .

All these practices and others similar are contrary to human dignity and the fundamental rights of all men. They degrade our civilization and are totally contrary to the plan of God. . . .

– Letter signed by the Episcopalian bishops,
sent to President Somoza January 8, 1977

I'm sure you've noticed my odd behavior over the past months. I no longer go to parties. I appear and disappear.

Dear Parents: This is because I've become a revolutionary, a member of the FSLN. I've done this for the following reasons: (1) For twenty years I have lived as I pleased and spent wildly while thousands of children, the sons of peasants and workers, suffered hunger, and died of malnutrition or in need of medical care. Our country is full of misery and backwardness. (2) All Nicaraguans have the sacred mission to fight for the freedom of our people. Our generation is doing what past generations should have done. Injustice and crime reign in the enslaved Nicaragua you have left us. We do not want our children to accuse us of the same thing. (3) The stench of the Somoza regime has become unbearable for the young. If our parents learned to live with this rotten government, we are prepared to risk our lives to put an end to it. (4) I am going to the mountains, where the patriots, the honest human beings, those who are willing to sacrifice everything for their people, can be found.

You should know that I am going of my own free will, without coercion and under no pressure from anyone. Forget the idea that someone is using me.

You will call me a bad son, but it is quite the contrary. You wanted me to be an honest man, and in Nicaragua, now, one can be honest only by fighting with all the forces against the Somoza tyranny, of which our people are so tired.

Please don't look for me, even less go to the security [police], because that would seriously endanger my life, since I am not willing to be caught alive if, because of you, they look for me and find me.

I send you each a kiss and an embrace. I thank you for your effort and sacrifice in making me a good man. Well, these efforts and sacrifice have borne fruit.

I am a revolutionary, which is "the highest rank to which a human being can aspire."

I send a kiss to Julio, to Maria Eugenia's children, to Federico and to Chico. Also to the maids.

I had hoped that our parting would not be painful, but circumstances have so determined it.

I, like Sandino, would like "a free country or death" and that is why I am going.

Embraces and kisses from your son who loves you more than ever. Until soon, that is, until victory.

Edgard

—A letter written by Edgard Lang Sacasa to his parents. His father, Federico Lang, was a wealthy Nicaraguan businessman and supporter of Somoza. Edgard was killed by the National Guard on April 16, 1979.

13

Marketplace in Diriamba

14

"Cuesta del Plomo," hillside outside Managua, a well known site of many assassinations carried out by the National Guard. People searched here daily for missing persons.

15

Wall graffiti on Somoza supporter's house burned in Monimbo, asking "Where is Norman González? The dictatorship must answer."

16

Residential neighborhood in Matagalpa

 17

Car of a Somoza informer burning in Managua

 **18**

Student demonstration broken up by the National Guard using tear gas, Managua, June 1978

Julio Buitrago died in combat . . . after hours of resistance. The Guard made the mistake of showing him fighting on television, creating a legend: showing Julio, alone, against three hundred Guards. . . . And all the people saw. . . .

— Omar Cabezas Lacayo, commander of the FSLN

. . . these good-byes are forever said Julio.
Bastards. After you saw the smoke and holes
*   opened by Sherman tanks through the house*
*   of the barrio Frixione. . . .*
Where he, alone, had fired against
*   hundreds of Guards, tanks, planes, security*
*   agents, trucks of reinforcements — firing*
*   alone from the balcony.*
He fired all afternoon. Intense firing from
*   both sides.*
And the tank with its cannon. Planes.
*   Helicopters. And they believed there were*
*   many, and it was one alone, it was him*
*   alone.*
The radio interrupted the news, and
*   advertised a soap.*

— Ernesto Cardenal, poet and priest.
From the poem "Oracle on Managua,"
on the death of Julio Buitrago, killed in
Managua July 15, 1969

In time the people began to come out into the streets. They made bonfires on every corner. You looked north, and there were bonfires; you looked south, and you saw more bonfires. There'd be bonfires in every direction. The Guard had lost control. They would arrive at a corner to put out one fire, and another would be lit at the next.

When the people sensed the Guard was coming, they would scatter into the nearest house. Once the Guard arrived, they would find all the doors closed and not know where anyone was. The *muchachos** by then would have escaped through the backyards.

— Damian, law student in Estelí

*Young boys in sympathy with the FSLN

I knew that they were fighting for us.
We were just living, eating, but those
of the Frente were following their
conscience. They understood that there
were some who ate and others who
didn't. They were fighting for those
who didn't.

— Cezar,
forty-five-year-old construction worker
in Managua

History doesn't come to an end,
with the ringing of bells by the grave,
or with the rumbling of tanks
against a peaceful city.

History begins when it is firmly established
that an ideal lives in a people,
though men die . . .

— Pedro Joaquín Chamorro,
editor of the opposition newspaper La Prensa.
Assassinated January 10, 1978

The Guard killed a small boy who had
built a bonfire with some other
children. Two hours later, the whole
town was in the streets, yelling.
People weren't afraid to go outside
any more. The army patrols arrived,
but no one ran away. We were
unarmed—just furious.

When we passed René Molina's
house—he was the Somozist
congressman we hated most in Estelí—
the paramilitary guards shot and
wounded a lot more people. The next
day, during the boy's burial, many
speeches were made, and people got so
angry they went and burned down
Molina's house. Then, more people
were arrested, and this caused more
demonstrations, because we knew that
going to jail was like being killed—
endless torture that was worse than
death. Every relative of every victim
was one more person against the Guard,
against the regime, against the system.

Somoza was trapped. He had to kill
us to stop us, but that only drove us on.

— Marta, housewife in Estelí

19

Burial of worker, with flag of
FSLN (Sandinista National
Liberation Front), in Diriamba

20

A funeral procession in
Jinotepe for assassinated
student leaders. Demonstrators
carry a photograph of Arlen
Siu, an FSLN guerrilla
fighter killed in the mountains
three years earlier.

21

Coffins of students being
carried in the streets of
Jinotepe

22

Motorcycle brigade, followed by a crowd of one hundred thousand people, leading Los Doce (The Twelve) *into Monimbo, July 5, 1978*

23

Youths practice throwing contact bombs in forest surrounding Monimbo

24

First day of popular insurrection, August 26, 1978

We are not military,
we are armed citizens. . . .

– General Augusto César Sandino, 1927

The kids used to throw firecrackers on Christmas Eve. An old man who made fireworks figured that if the tiny bomb worked, by adding more explosives to make it bigger he could produce a real explosion and destroy things. That's how the contact bomb was born. It was the only defense we had.

He would sell them at a dollar apiece. We used to buy them, but as the struggle continued and we got more experience, we came to realize he was exploiting us. We told him to make them cheaper and join up with us. So he did, and then he showed us how to make the bomb ourselves.

– Justo,
father of three, shoemaker of Monimbo

To make a bomb, you need gun powder, chlorate, and sugar. You mix it all up and add shrapnel — pieces of glass, steel, and pebbles. Then you wrap it in newspaper, dry it, and seal it with masking tape.

It was so simple anyone could do it. Our worst problem was finding the chlorate, so we used to send a lady to the drugstore to buy it. She would bring it back under the vegetables she carried on her head, and the Guard never stopped her. But when the dictatorship banned its sale, we had to raid the drugstores.

– Sylvia Reyes, mother of two,
organizer of neighborhood women
in Managua

It was at the time when the Frente had done everything. Nothing more remained to do except something so that the world would know what was happening in Nicaragua. . . .

I'm not sure if it was in '70 or '71, but I remember it was at the time when the Frente had such limited resources, that we had spent three days almost not eating, we didn't even have enough for cigarettes. . . . We'd fed ourselves with turtles we'd caught fishing and iguanas we'd hunted. At that time we were in Leon, at the house of a family from Subtiava, Oscar Turcios, Pedro Arauz, and Ricardo Morales. . . . They're all dead now.

It was one night when again we had nothing for supper, and so we went to bed with a glass thick with coffee. I tell you, sometimes hunger does wonders. Maybe it was the combination of black coffee on an empty stomach that didn't let me sleep all night long. I was just thinking about where to get money to eat, when the idea of the Palace came to me. During that night I planned how it could be done. Very early, at 5 A.M. I woke the others, shaking each by the feet, and then when they were all up I asked them how many millions of dollars they wanted, 10, 15, 20? Then I presented them with the plan that became known as Operation "Rigoberto López Pérez."

– Eden Pastora, known as Commander "Zero," FSLN commander in charge of the taking of the National Palace, August 22, 1978; named after the poet who killed Somoza's father in 1956

It was the day when they started banging the pots in the neighborhood. The day when the Guard thought the Sandinistas were armed to the teeth. But we had only one .22 all night long: the pots were making the racket. And it was that day that I felt powerful with only one little pistol—I'd never had a weapon before. Later I understood that the Guard had weapons, but they didn't have courage, nor cause, nor ideal.

– Enrique Cano, fifteen-year-old boy living in Managua

Muchachos *(young rebels) holding barricade in Matagalpa*

25

Awaiting counterattack by the Guard in Matagalpa

26

Muchacho *wearing Spider Man mask in Masaya, September 1978*

27

28

Young boy killed during fighting; wall behind reads, "National Guard get out of Monimbo. The people are dying because of Somoza."

29

Estelí, the fifth day of continuous bombing, September 1978

30

National Guard entering Estelí

The person who expects of his country not even a plot of earth for his grave, deserves to be listened to and not only listened to, but to be believed. . . .

—Augusto César Sandino

The first time we saw planes in the sky was that September. They were firing rockets, and we thought we were going to die. We heard this *pra-pra-pra* sound. We crouched down, looking for somewhere to hide, and my stomach churned, my whole body shook, just looking at the beast flying over us.

The Guardsmen in the town told the planes where to fire—which street, which house. We heard all the conversations over the radio. They said, "The hospital's ours, the barracks are ours, the rest is just meat. Exterminate them!"

When they described a house—say, it was such and such a color—we knew there were *compañeros** there, so we'd send someone to warn them immediately.

—Irma, housewife from Matagalpa

*Used in reference to partisans

Estelí was no more. The dead were in the streets and in the houses. There was no water, no light. There was hunger because people could not buy food. There wasn't any.

−Carlos,
professor from Estelí

Seizing government
construction truck in Masaya

I have always believed that we must first exhaust all non-violent means. That we must use non-violence actively, within the bounds of civil society. But I must recognize what some moral and theological authorities believe, that collective armed resistance is acceptable when the following three conditions are fulfilled:

1) the existence of a self-evident injustice of extreme gravity that would legitimize an undisputed situation of self-defense;

2) the proven failure of all concrete peaceful solutions;

3) that armed struggle caused by injustice will cause less suffering than the perpetuation of that injustice.

−Archbishop of Managua, Msgr. Miguel
Obando y Bravo, La Prensa, *February 9, 1978*

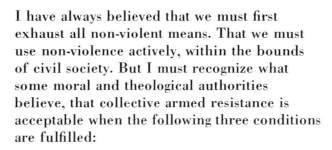

Muchacho *withdrawing from*
commercial district of Masaya
after three days of bombing

Townspeople taking goods
from burned-out store in Estelí

34

Fleeing the bombing to seek refuge outside of Estelí

35

Monimbo woman carrying her dead husband home to be buried in their backyard

36

Body being burned by the Red Cross to prevent the spread of disease, Masaya

In León that day, people were running along the street, screaming: "The Guard's going to burn down the whole neighborhood— everybody out! They're going to start shelling!" Then the Guard turned up and started shooting through the doors, shouting and trying to smash them down.

All my neighbors ran out, mothers with their kids in their arms, old people stumbling along. We didn't know what to do or where to go. We were afraid of crossing the railroad tracks because on the other side, in the bushes of the empty lots, there was a whole army with tanks and tractors.

Suddenly, some Guardsmen came out of the bushes and stopped us. They lined up a group of about twenty-five men, young and old, made them lie down on the ground, and searched them. Then they told them to kneel down. And then just one Guard machine-gunned them down.

In my street alone, twenty-two people of all ages were killed. They were humble and peaceful people.

Their names and ages were:

Carlos Hernández, 20 years old
Gonzalo Hernández, 30 years old
Miguel Centeno, 32 years old
Julio Páiz Berrera, 27 years old
Flavio Páiz Barrera, 18 years old
Clemente Páiz Barrera, 23 years old
Pedro Vargas Alvarez, 29 years old
Luis A. Martínez Alvarez, 24 years old
Hilario Martínez Ramírez, 50 years old
Julio Lezana Alvarez, 30 years old
Salvador Vílchez Poveda, 23 years old
Pedro Vílchez Poveda, 17 years old
Ernesto Luna Ruiz, 27 years old
Gonzalo Luna Ruiz, 25 years old
Porfirio Páiz Altamirano, 25 years old
Víctor Torrez Pineda, 19 years old
Pedro Pérez Paoilla, 21 years old
Luis Vargas Parajón, 24 years old
Róger González Bermúdez, 25 years old
Jesús Padilla Reyes, 19 years old
Julio Páiz, 25 years old
Manuel Coca Salazar, 20 years old

—Anonymous testimony given before the Inter-American Commission on Human Rights, November 1978

I'd seen perhaps the most humiliated, the most miserable, the most oppressed of Nicaragua. I tried to respond in a Christian way, peacefully, promoting social and human development; looking for ways to help these people live better by their own means and with government resources. But I realized that it was all a lie, all deceit. . . .

I became discouraged to see that so much work had meant nothing, that so many hopes were left in the air. The people continued living the same. . . .

And so I joined the armed struggle, knowing that nothing peaceful was possible . . . any other way would have been dishonest to my people and myself. . . .

—Father Gasper García Laviana,
Spanish priest of the Sacred Heart Order,
who died in combat on December 9, 1978

Imagine shooting, for example. I mean—I used to organize people in my neighborhood, and now I had to start shooting, killing. I'd never done that before.

Imagine how I felt. I had to be firm with myself and decide I had to start. You stop and you think for a moment; then you remember the women raped by the Guard, the friends who died, and your country, waiting. And you say: we've got to fight; we've got to stay alive.

You understand? Individual violence is one thing; but when a whole people turns to violence, it becomes a part of history.

—El Ciego,
university student

Returning home, Masaya,
September 1978

Toward Sandinista training
camp in the mountains north
of Estelí

Breakfast, rice

40

Woman instructor teaching marksmanship to woman volunteer

41

Guard patrol in Masaya beginning house-to-house search for Sandinistas

42

Searching everyone traveling by car, truck, bus, or foot

FROM: Regional Headquarters "Commandante Julio Buitrago Urroz" (FSLN)
TO: The People of Nicaragua

Our squads have carried out the following operations:

—November 16:   The Urania Zelaya Ubeda squad carried out an operation, recovering medicine from the Linda Vista Drugstore.

—November 19:   The Urania Zelaya Ubeda squad distributed propaganda on the Route 5 bus. The *compañeros* passed out leaflets and urged the passengers to join the struggle.

—November 20:   The Igor Ubeda squad in an action named "We don't sell out or surrender" appropriated arms from the home of National Guard Sergeant Molina, who works in the traffic section at Police Headquarters. The operation was carried out at 17:25 and the following items were taken:
  2 first aid manuals
  1 single-shot 12 gauge shotgun
  1 semi-automatic .22 caliber rifle
  4 pairs of National Guard boots
  .22 and 9mm ammunition and .12 gauge cartridges
  screwdrivers for dismantling weapons
  photos and a passport belonging to the National Guardsman

  Graffiti and leaflets with Sandinista slogans were left in the house.

—November 21: The José Benito Escobar squad carried out a recovery operation in the shop Diana, neighborhood of Monseñor Lezcano. Its purpose was to take watches for our brothers in the mountains. They distributed propaganda and explained the aims of the organization to the salesmen.

—Extracts from FSLN communiqué
December 1978

Journalist: If the National Guard comes to you and says, "General, we want you to leave!" will you leave?
Pres. Somoza: No.
Journalist: Couldn't they force you to do so?
Pres. Somoza: Maybe I could use force against them.
Journalist: But they have the weapons.
Pres. Somoza: But I have the people. . . .

—CBS-TV News interview,
December 17, 1978

We don't accept the mediation of the government of the United States in the internal conflicts of our country. With what moral authority can the U.S. government come and propose a mediation when it is with the weapons that the gringos sell the Somoza government that our people are being murdered in the streets, mountains, and cities of the country; the bombs dropped on Matagalpa as well as the planes are made in the U.S. The tear gas, M-16 rifles, the equipment used by the Nicaraguan army is produced in the United States. It is the military aid of the U.S. to Somoza which continues to maintain Somoza in power.

—Dora Maria Tellez,
twenty-two-year-old FSLN
commander, November 1978

After September, we knew we had to get better organized. So we started preparing for the next insurrection by setting up Civil Defense Committees on each block, trying to get first-aid kits for every street where we had clandestine clinics for the fighters. It was a lot of work. You had to find safe houses for storing medicine, food supplies, and arms. We couldn't meet openly. We had to do things one at a time, house by house—pretending we were just dropping over to the neighbor's for coffee. I watched how they were and then decided whether we could trust them.

But we knew pretty much who the Somoza informers were. Many of them wore high lace-up boots, which the Guard gave them, or yellow *guayabera* shirts with four pockets.

—Julia,
mother of three, neighborhood organizer
in Managua

43

Guard on daily patrol in the countryside, February 1979

44

Paramilitary forces, as extension of National Guard, search for weapons

45

Wall calling for a popular democratic government by the MPU (United People's Movement)

46

Waiting at the central police station headquarters for missing relatives, Managua

47

Popular forces begin final offensive in Masaya, June 8, 1979

48

National Guardsmen trapped on main street of Masaya

The people of Monimbo believed that the Sandinistas would come from somewhere else in Nicaragua. We wanted them to think that because we were organizing clandestinely. We painted slogans on the walls saying FSLN, WE'RE WAITING FOR YOU HERE IN MONIMBO or FSLN, YOUR PEOPLE ARE CALLING FOR YOU TO COME.

Even during the September insurrection, many townspeople didn't realize who the Sandinistas were. But by June the town began to understand that the sons and daughters of Monimbo were also the Sandinistas.

– Augusto,
taxidriver of Monimbo

There was constant tension: "It's coming this weekend" or "It's coming next month—it'll be the fifth."
People lived by rumors.

All we did was get people out of jail. The repression was incredible. The National Guard pulled people out of their houses, put their shirts over their heads—so all we'd see in the back of the Becat [jeep]* was this naked kid with his head forced down, and we couldn't tell who it was. People just disappeared and there was nothing we could do. Everybody was waiting. That was the worst part. People were saying anything is better than waiting. Why don't they come?

– Sister Juliana,
Maryknoll nun living in Managua

*Spanish jeep used for anti-terrorist operations, known by its orange color and machine-gun mount

The smell of gunpowder was in the air, the smell of war. The people were expecting us. So was the Guard. We fought inch by inch and street by street to take Estelí again.

The Guard set up fortified stations on practically every block, in schools, stores, pharmacies, even churches, with up to thirty men at each one. We began our advance at one house where, I remember, the owners had run out so fast they left a pot of beans soaking on the patio. We crossed the backyard, dragging ourselves on our bellies and running from tree to tree. After we broke a hole through the back wall, we were right next to the Guard's position. It seemed like the entire world had gone silent.

– Fernando, twenty-two-year-old civilian

Whenever we took a town, the whole population came out to watch. Then we called for new recruits, encouraging those who wanted to leave with us to train, right there on the street. We taught them to shoot — lying down, kneeling, squatting, standing up, leaning forward, leaning back — then to assemble and dismantle weapons, as well as some fighting tactics. We never lacked people. Only arms.

– Omar Cabezas

49

National Guard reinforcements entering Masaya beseiged by FSLN

50

Muchachos take over neighborhood and put on captured National Guard uniforms, Managua, June 1979

51

Street fighter in Managua

52

Sandinistas distributing arms captured from the National Guard garrison in Matagalpa

53

Population of San Isidro and Sandinistas after surrender of local National Guard, June 13, 1979

54

Serving food to Sandinistas holding the barricades in Managua

The first day, when people said, "They're coming—they've taken the neighborhood," we ran out and helped litter the streets with bottles, garbage—anything—so the Guard's tanks could not enter. All the neighbors were doing it. I was nervous but very happy too. I walked from corner to corner carrying bricks on my head to help build barricades. At night, the *muchachos* waited behind them. They were expecting an attack at any moment and had to keep awake, so everyone brought them coffee, crackers, anything. It was food we'd put aside for the war, but now we shared it with the *muchachos*.

—Rosa Alilia,
housewife in Managua

That afternoon we gathered our military leaders and told them of the decision to withdraw from Managua to Masaya. Their first reactions were negative; they argued that we couldn't abandon the people who had gone into the streets with so much trust. Our decision would leave them at the mercy of the enemy. "If we lose, we die, but we die with the people." This was understandable coming from a group of popular leaders, it was difficult for them to see it was a military move, a tactical problem, not just a moral problem. They began to understand and we planned the withdrawal.

The groups began to move in columns of two men; people got hold of whatever they could and fell into line, beginning to walk not even knowing where they were going. And so it grew. "Where are we going?"—"We're leaving"—"I'm not going to stay here, they'll kill us, I'm going too."

The first group began to leave at six-thirty in the evening and the last at one that morning. The column advanced like an immense snake. At the beginning it was more or less cohesive, but at the back it was chaos. Each group had organized itself. What everyone had in mind was "Masaya, Masaya." In Masaya there was food . . . Masaya was liberated territory . . . the *compas** were there . . . the future was there . . . life was there.

—Joaquín Cuadra,
commander of the FSLN Internal Front

*short for *compañeros*

55

Sandinista in a home in Estelí

56

Sandinistas in the streets of Estelí

57

One hour after the taking of San Isidro

58

Sandinistas on daily rounds in Estelí neighborhood

59

Neighborhood bomb shelter dug under street in anticipation of renewed air attacks, Managua, June 1979

60

Children rescued from a house destroyed by 1,000-pound bomb dropped in Managua. They died shortly after.

The *Frente* gave us leaflets telling us how to make bomb shelters. We have twelve children, so my husband made us all squat down two by two in the living room, to make sure we would all fit. We dug it there—five yards wide and three yards deep. We put wooden planks and corrugated iron sheeting over the top and used parts of the kids' iron bed frames as supports. We didn't want to die just because we hadn't made it right.

At five the next morning, the neighbors started screaming that a rocket had fallen nearby. The shrapnel ripped apart a door across the street. It was awful. We spent the whole day just counting the mortars fall.

—Rosa Alilia

In Diriamba during the war a town assembly was formed to decide on a representative council—it was pretty much the first people's government. Everyone had to get used to making decisions beyond little routine things.

People were all in favor and it seemed like a great idea, but they weren't used to discussing things collectively and coming to an agreement. When a meeting ended, the crowd would continue the discussion in the street, thinking someone would solve the problems. They thought the answers would come from above. That was the hardest thing to work against.

—Milagros,
civil servant and member
of the FSLN

At nightfall, when the Guard stopped fighting, we rested, checked our guns, ammunition, and boots. You lit up a cigarette and smoked it lying down, the tip to the ground. Otherwise, you could get shot smack in the face.

On watch, alone with your gun behind the barricade, you get to thinking a whole lot of things. You remember your family, the good times, and think about what it'll be like when Somoza and the Guard are gone, when there are no more bullets, when there's nothing but progress.

Suddenly, you hear the whistle of a bullet. You get up, look around, and see a friend alongside. He's asleep and you have to watch over him. Then someone brings you a cup of coffee. And another cigarette.

—*Fernando*

National Guards taken prisoner-of-war in Sebaco

Sandinista barricade during last days of fighting in Matagalpa

Final assault on the Estelí National Guard headquarters, July 16, 1979

64

Sandinistas at the walls of the Estelí National Guard headquarters

65

Body of National Guardsman, killed during the taking of Jinotepe, being burned with the official state portrait of President Somoza

66

On the road to Managua

Anastasio Somoza, ex-President of Nicaragua, after abandoning the country, was admitted to the United States with a tourist and business visa, valid for four years.

Somoza, upon arrival, stated that he was happy to be back in the country where he had lived so many years as a student and businessman. He said that he would return to Nicaragua the day his people called him back, and that otherwise he would remain in exile for the rest of his life. . . .

– Radio Sandino, July 17, 1979

It was eleven in the morning. The planes full of Guards were taking off one by one. The radio kept repeating that the Guards were laying down their guns, that they were leaving. I could feel it everywhere — victory.

But I was still waiting for my boys to come home. Many others had already shown up. It was eleven o'clock, and I hadn't even made the coffee or the breakfast or anything.

Then some kids ran in shouting, "Doña María! Henry's coming!" I hadn't seen or heard from him for days and days, and there he was, marching down the other side of the street. I was crazy with happiness, blowing him kisses in the air. Half an hour later Javier, the second one, turned up, riding a jeep painted FREE COUNTRY OR DEATH. I cried out to him too.

But there was still one missing — my youngest. I went inside, wringing my hands and thinking, "My baby's missing! They've killed my little boy!" Everyone from the neighborhood had appeared, all but my little one. I went outside again and watched and waited. Someone said they saw Enrique coming, riding a tank, others said no, it wasn't him. I was afraid it wasn't the truth. Then suddenly I saw him. He was coming. I ran over, held him, touched him, embraced him. It seemed impossible that he had come!

– María Cano, housewife in Managua

Victory has a price both costly and sad.
The joy brought by that triumph
is the inheritance of the future generations;
It is for them that we do battle. . . .

– Carlos Fonseca, founder of the FSLN,
killed in battle November 7, 1976

A lot of time is spent trying to label this revolution. But we know that names can't make revolutions.

People want to define whether it's Communist pro-Soviet or Communist pro-Cuban, or Social Democrat, or Eurocommunist, or whatever . . . it's Sandinista. . . . We don't claim we've invented anything, but we are trying to give this process some new dimension, a local quality, if not a universal one. We don't claim to substitute universal doctrines, but we do claim the right to lead this process along a truly creative path. It seems to me that a revolution that doesn't begin by being creative is not a revolution.

– Sergio Ramirez, writer, university professor,
and member of Junta for Government of National
Reconstruction, November 1979

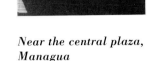

67

Near the central plaza,
Managua

68

Entering the central plaza in
Managua to celebrate victory,
July 20, 1979

69

In the central plaza, renamed
Plaza de la Revolucion

70

Father collecting remains of assassinated son, identified by a shoe lying nearby

71

Wall, Managua

THE PARROTS

My friend Michel is the officer in
  charge of Somoto,
there, by the border with Honduras,
where they caught, he told me,
  contraband parrots
about to be exported to the United States
where they would learn to speak English.
There were one hundred eighty-six parrots,
  and forty-seven had already died in their cages.
And he returned them to the place from
  which they had come
And just as the truck was arriving at
  a place called "The Plains"
close to the mountains where the parrots once lived
(the mountains seemed huge behind those plains)
  the parrots became agitated and began to
  flap their wings,
pushing against the walls of their cages.
And when the cages were opened
they all flew like arrows toward their mountains.
That's just what the Revolution did with
  us, I think:
took us out of the cages in which we
  were being carried off to speak English.
And sent us back to the land from which we
  had been pulled.
The green compas like parrots
  gave back to the parrots their green mountains.
But forty-seven had died.

— Poem by Ernesto Cardenal

1524 Spanish conquistadors fight and defeat the Indians, naming the newly conquered land "Nicaragua" after the Indian chief Nicarao.

1821 Nicaragua becomes independent.

1855 North American adventurer William Walker invades Nicaragua, imposing slavery and declaring himself president. He was overthrown two years later.

1893 The Liberal party government led by José Santos Zelaya begins a process of modernization and national development.

1909 President Zelaya refuses to grant canal rights to the United States. The U.S. State Department supports a revolt by the Conservative party, which in return agrees to permanent U.S. military presence. U.S. banks take control of Nicaraguan finances, railroads, and communications.

1912 U.S. Marines remain in the country to support the
–1926 Conservative government, which is faced with continuous armed Liberal rebellions.

The Bryan-Chamorro Treaty is signed, giving the United States perpetual rights for the construction of an interoceanic canal through Nicaragua.

1927 The Liberal leaders surrender and sign a U.S.-supervised peace treaty. Only General Augusto César

Sandino refuses to comply. He assembles an army of peasants and launches a guerrilla war against the U.S. occupational forces, which is to last seven years, during which the United States experimented with its first aerial bombardment techniques.

1933 Unable to crush Sandino's army and faced by growing domestic criticism of U.S. involvement in Nicaragua, the marines are withdrawn. They are replaced by a new army and police force, the National Guard, trained and equipped by the U.S., to be headed by U.S.-appointed Anastasio "Tacho" Somoza Garcia.

1934 Sandino signs for peace with the new president, Sacasa, and returns to the northern mountains to continue organizing peasant cooperatives begun during the war. On February 21 Sandino is assassinated on the orders of Tacho Somoza.

1936 Somoza ousts Sacasa and takes the presidency.

1947 Following U.S. pressure to hold elections, a new president, Leonard Argüello, is elected. After twenty-eight days in office, he is overthrown by Somoza, who then installs his uncle as the next president.

1951 A pact is signed between Somoza's Liberal party and the Conservatives, allowing Somoza's election as president.

1956   After over twenty years of rule, Anastasio Somoza
        Garcia is executed by a poet, Rigoberto López Pérez.
        His son, Luis, replaces his father as president, and his
        second son, Anastasio, or "Tachito," takes over as
        Commander-in-Chief of the Armed Forces. A period
        of brutal repression begins.

1958   A number of armed movements develop, with
–1960   differing political origins and no single direction.
        Some are led by the veterans of Sandino, some by
        members of the middle class, such as newspaper
        editor Pedro Joaquín Chamorro, who at this time
        stages an armed invasion, which fails to take power.

1961   The Sandinista National Liberation Front (FSLN) is
        founded by Carlos Fonseca, Tomás Borge, and Silvio
        Mayorga, and combines several of the existing armed
        movements.

        Somoza offers Nicaragua as a base for the CIA-backed
        invasion of Cuba's Bay of Pigs.

1963   The first guerrilla actions of the FSLN are taken in
        the zone of Rio Bocay.

        The United States, with a new strategy for social and
        economic development in Latin America known as
        the Alliance for Progress, pressures Somoza to form a
        civilian government. Rene Schick is picked to be the
        next "elected" president.

1964   Somoza, in response to continuing resistance,
        collaborates in the creation of the Central American
        Defense Council (CONDECA).

1965   National Guard troops are sent to support U.S.
        Marines in the invasion of the Dominican Republic.

1967   During Anastasio "Tachito" Somoza Debayle's
        presidential campaign, hundreds of people
        demonstrating support for a Conservative opposition
        candidate, Fernando Agüero, are killed by the
        National Guard. Somoza is accused of electoral
        fraud. He becomes president and continues command
        of the Armed Forces. Agüero negotiates with Somoza
        to gain seats in the National Congress.

        The FSLN sets up a rural base in Pancasan, where
        guerrilla actions intensify.

1972   An earthquake destroys the capital, Managua, killing
        15,000 people and leaving 170,000 homeless. Incoming
        relief supplies are found on the black market.
        International aid is used to expand the business
        empire of the Somoza family, which takes advantage
        of reconstruction needs by making land and
        construction deals and eliminating the private sector
        from investment opportunities.

1974   Somoza becomes president for another seven-year
        term, in an election boycotted by the major
        opposition parties.

        The FSLN stages an assault on a Somocista Christmas
        party, taking twelve Nicaraguan diplomats and
        government members hostage. Somoza accedes to
        FSLN demands for $1 million ransom, release of
        political prisoners, and the press and radio
        publication of an FSLN statement.

UDEL (Democratic Union for Liberation), a broad alliance of political parties, businessmen, and unions, is organized and headed by Pedro Joaquín Chamorro.

1975   A country-wide counterinsurgency campaign is launched against the FSLN.

1976   Carlos Fonseca, founder of the FSLN, is killed in combat with the National Guard, and Tomás Borge, co-founder, is jailed and put in solitary confinement.

Nicaraguan Catholic Church Bishops and U.S. missionaries denounce National Guard repression against peasants, documenting the "disappearance" of several village communities in the north.

1977   Somoza lifts martial law and censorship following U.S. threats to cut off military assistance if human rights are not respected.

The Sandinistas simultaneously attack three National Guard garrisons: San Carlos in the south, Ocotal in the north, and Masaya near the capital.

"Los Doce" (The Twelve), a newly formed group of prominent businessmen, churchmen, and intellectuals, calls for unified opposition to Somoza, including participation of the FSLN.

The Archbishop attempts to organize a "national dialogue" with Somoza.

1/78   Pedro Joaquín Chamorro is assassinated. 100,000 people demonstrate and follow his coffin in a funeral procession through Managua. A national general strike is organized by the businessmen and UDEL, demanding the resignation of Somoza. It lasts ten days.

The business sector organizes a new opposition party, the MDN (Nicaraguan Democratic Movement).

2/78   The FSLN attacks the cities of Granada and Rivas.

National Guard tear gas a mass honoring Pedro Joaquín Chamorro in Monimbo. The Indian community builds barricades and trenches overnight, and rises up in the first popular rebellion against Somoza.

3/78   Demonstrations are held by neighborhood committees for better transportation and living conditions.

5/78   A hunger strike for Tomás Borge and Marcio Jean is supported by the women's movement AMPRONAC, demanding improved prison conditions and an end to their solitary confinement.

The Broad Opposition Front (FAO) is formed, uniting "Los Doce," UDEL, and other opposition parties.

6/78   Secondary schools and universities are boycotted in a national strike by 30,000 students and teachers.

7/78   Members of "Los Doce" returning to Nicaragua from self-exile are met by an estimated crowd of 100,000 supporters.

The United People's Movement (MPU) is formed as a coalition of unions and grassroots organizations linked to the FSLN.

8/78   Led by Commander Eden Pastora, the Sandinistas storm the National Palace and take sixty-seven Congressmen and 1,000 government officials hostage, forcing Somoza to release fifty-nine political prisoners, publish the FSLN program, and pay ransom.

The FAO calls for a second general strike, with no definite duration. The entire country is paralyzed.

A popular uprising begins in the town of Matagalpa.

9/78   The Sandinistas simultaneously attack the towns of León, Masaya, Chinandega, and Estelí, and the neighborhoods of Las Americas and Open 3 in Managua. They are supported by a popular insurrection. A state of seige is decreed throughout the country. After several days of fighting, the rebel cities are finally retaken, one by one, by the National Guard after extensive aerial bombardment. According to the Red Cross, the September fighting left 5,000 dead. Approximately 100,000 people seek refuge in the neighboring countries of Honduras and Costa Rica.

10/78   The Organization of American States (OAS) sends in an international team, headed by William Bowdler of the United States, to mediate between Somoza and the FAO, and define conditions for a post-Somoza Nicaragua.

11/78   Somoza refuses to leave, and the mediators attempt to involve Somoza's Liberal party in the talks. "Los Doce" reject the mediation, stating they cannot endorse "Somocismo without Somoza," a plan that would leave structures like the National Guard or the Liberal party intact. A plebiscite is suggested by the U.S. to determine if Somoza should continue or leave the country. Somoza rejects the proposal.

The Inter-American Commission for Human Rights of the OAS visits Nicaragua and publishes a report that condemns the Somoza regime for having committed "genocide."

Somoza doubles strength of the National Guard to an estimated 15,000 and turns to Argentina and Israel for arms supplies when U.S. military cutoffs restrict direct sales.

Civil Defense Committees, sponsored by the MPU, organize in the city neighborhoods, preparing people for wartime defense. They stockpile food and medicine, give training in first aid.

2/79   A National Patriotic Front (FPN) is formed, combining the MPU with members of FAO who reject mediation efforts.

3/79   The FSLN announces internal unification.

4/79   The FSLN launches the "final offensive," taking
–   Estelí and Jinotega in the north, initiating guerrilla
5/79   activities in the Atlantic coast area, and waging frontal attacks along the Costa Rican border in the south, including the towns of Rivas and El Naranjo.

6/4/79   A general strike brings the country to a standstill. The

FSLN continues guerrilla actions in the north and conventional warfare in the south. The population of the major cities—León, Matagalpa, Chinandega, Estelí, Masaya, and the eastern part of the capital, Managua—rise up against Somoza. Fighting also begins in smaller surrounding towns.

6/13/79   San Isidro is liberated.

6/15/79   The frontier post of Penas Blancas is taken.

6/16/79   A five-member provisional government of National Reconstruction is named by the Sandinistas, including members of the FSLN, MPU, the business community, and the moderate opposition.

Ecuador, Mexico, Peru, Brazil, and Panama break diplomatic relations with Somoza's government.

6/21/79   The U.S. calls for an emergency session of the OAS. Its proposal to send an inter-American "peacekeeping force" to Nicaragua is defeated, an unprecedented decision. A resolution is drawn up calling for Somoza's immediate resignation.

ABC-TV correspondent Bill Stewart is shot dead by a National Guardsman in Managua. Film footage is shown worldwide.

6/24/79   Chichigalpa becomes the second liberated town.

6/25/79   The FSLN withdraws from Managua after nineteen days of resistance, reestablishing its forces in Masaya.

In the "liberated areas" of Nicaragua, the MPU organizes people to prepare for a long war by sowing crops and starting up production for basic needs. Local assemblies are formed by popular vote in many towns.

7/1/79   Somoza fails in an attempt to enlist military support of CONDECA, the Central American Defense Force.

7/2/79   The Voice of America announces twenty-two cities held by the Sandinistas.

7/9/79   León, the second largest city, is declared liberated.

The U.S. pressures the provisional government to add two more conservative members and to preserve the National Guard.

7/16/79   Estelí is declared liberated. The Sandinistas, having taken a series of towns—Jinotepe, Juigalpa, Sebaco, Rivas—control major road access and begin their march to Managua.

7/17/79   Somoza resigns and flies to Miami with his family and chiefs of staff, carrying the coffins of his father and brother.

The provisional government arrives in León and holds its first press conference.

The interim president, Francisco Urcuyo, orders National Guard troops to keep fighting and refuses to hand over power. While some fighting continues on the southern front and in Matagalpa, the National Guard surrender in Somoto, Boaco, and Granada. Fleeing deserters hijack Red Cross and Nicaraguan Air Force planes.

Urcuyo flees the country after thirty-six hours in office.

7/19/79   The Sandinista columns converge on the capital, ending a war that, according to the United Nations Economic Committee on Latin America (CEPAL) report, left: 40,000 dead (1.5 percent of the population); 40,000 children orphaned; 200,000 families homeless; 750,000 persons dependent on food assistance; 70 percent of the main export, cotton, not planted; 33 percent of all industrial property destroyed; $1.5 billion worth of physical damage; and an external debt of $1.6 billion.

7/20/79   The provisional government and the National Direction of the FSLN, along with Sandinista columns, are welcomed at Managua's central plaza by a crowd of 200,000.